The
Science of
Success

Written and published by: KingDavid Clarett

Giving acknowledgment and thanks to:

Cadence Eikenberry, for not only designing the book cover but also for embracing the challenge of stepping out of her comfort zone to create a greater version of herself. Her willingness to grow and evolve is a reflection of the very themes explored in this book. The elegance and creativity she brought to the cover perfectly encapsulate the journey of self-discovery and transformation that lies within these pages.

Her personal growth is a living testimony to the stories I share with you. It serves as a powerful reminder that you do not have to be great to start, but you do have to start to be great. I am deeply grateful for her contribution, which goes far beyond the visual—it embodies the spirit of this book.

"The Science Of Success: A Guide to True Success"

In "Finding Your Path: A Guide to True Success," you'll embark on a transformative journey towards realizing your true potential and achieving meaningful success. This book delves into the essential principles and practices that lead to a fulfilling life, emphasizing that success is not just about dreaming but about taking consistent, deliberate action.

Key Themes:

1. What Do You Want?
   - Discovering your true desires and setting clear goals is the first step towards creating the life you want. Like an inventor solving a problem, you must define your destination before embarking on your journey.

2. Glow in the Dark: The Power of Hard Work
   - Success often comes from working hard, even when no one is watching. This chapter highlights the importance of perseverance, integrity, and always striving to leave a positive impact.

3. Successfully Uncomfortable: Growth Outside Your Comfort Zone
   - True growth occurs when you step outside your comfort zone. Just like a plant outgrowing a small pot, you need to expand your horizons to reach your full potential.

4. Your Word is Your Bond: Reliability and Trust
   - Being reliable and keeping your promises builds your reputation and trustworthiness. Your word is a powerful tool; use it wisely and consistently.

5. Failing is Not Losing: Embracing Failure as Part of Success
   - Failure is not the end but a step towards success. Learning from mistakes and persisting despite setbacks are crucial for achieving your goals.

6. Dangerous Mind: The Power of a Positive Mindset
   - A positive mindset is a powerful ally. Surround yourself with supportive friends and keep negativity at bay to maintain your confidence and motivation.

7. Predict the Future: Creating Your Own Path
   - The best way to predict the future is to create it. Stop reacting to life and start making intentional choices that lead to your desired outcomes.

8. Golden Clock: Valuing Time Over Money
   - Time is your most valuable resource. Use it wisely, as it cannot be replenished. Prioritize meaningful activities that align with your goals.

9. Be Prepared: Seizing Opportunities
   - Preparation is key to making the most of opportunities. Equip yourself with the right skills, knowledge, and tools to be ready when opportunities arise.

10. Closed Mouths: The Importance of Asking Questions
    - Never be afraid to ask questions. Seeking knowledge and clarification prevents mistakes and leads to better decisions and outcomes.

11. I'm Exhausted: The Balance Between Rest and Action
    - Taking breaks is essential for rejuvenation, but balance is crucial. Rest enough to recover but not so much that you lose momentum.

12. Goals VR Dreams: Turning Aspirations into Reality
    - Goals without action are just dreams. Take concrete steps to pursue your goals and turn your aspirations into tangible achievements.

13. Be Yourself: Authenticity and True Success
    - True success is personal. Live authentically, follow your own path, and find what truly fills you with joy and purpose.

Introduction: The Beginning of Your New Journey

Welcome to the beginning of your new journey in finding the science of success. This book aims to guide you through the principles and practices necessary to achieve true success. What we want in life may be easy to see, but how we get there is a whole different story. I must warn you, this book is not for everyone. It's not a get-rich-quick solution or an easy money scheme. You will have to put in the work to reap the benefits.

Success is a deeply personal concept, and everyone has a different vision of it. Some may seek fame, others fortune. Some may desire to be a mother or a wife who stays at home and raises the kids, while others aspire to be a husband and father who can easily provide for his family's needs. Whatever your definition of success, this book provides the secrets to unlocking the science of success.

Throughout these pages, you'll discover that success is not just about dreaming but about taking consistent, deliberate action. This book will offer you valuable insights, practical advice, and actionable steps to help you create the life you want. By embracing these lessons and putting them to use, you'll be well on your way to achieving your unique vision of success. So, get ready to embark on this transformative journey. Remember, the path to success is not always easy, but with dedication and perseverance, you can reach your goals and live a fulfilling, successful life.

Chapter One: What Do You Want?

Like any good inventor, we must ask ourselves: What are we going to create? An inventor identifies a problem and devises a solution. In life, you must determine what you want to achieve. Having a clear destination is essential.

When you leave your house to go to the store, you know exactly where the store is. If you don't, you use a GPS to find it. If you lack a GPS, you ask for directions. The point is, you know where you want to go.

So, where do you want to be in life? Are you willing to do what it takes to get there?

Finding Your Place

Finding your place in life starts with understanding where you are now. Reflect on what you have and what you appreciate about your current situation. For instance, I love my job as a home health aide. The connections with my clients bring me joy, and the work feels meaningful. However, like many people, I feel underpaid. My desire to provide better for my family drives me to seek new opportunities.

Assessing Your Current Situation

Take stock of your current life:

1. What do you love about your life? For me, it's the fulfillment from helping others and the connections I build with my clients.
2. What do you want to improve? Personally, I want to improve my financial situation to spend more quality time with my family and afford activities for them.
3. What resources do you have? Consider your skills, experiences, and the people who support you.

Setting Your Goals

Once you understand where you are, think about where you want to go. Goals give you a sense of direction. They are like your destination when you set out from your house. Without them, you might find yourself wandering aimlessly.

1. Short-Term Goals: These are stepping stones. For me, a short-term goal might be exploring higher-paying job opportunities or additional training to enhance my qualifications.
2. Long-Term Goals: These are your ultimate destinations. My long-term goal is to achieve financial stability, allowing more family time and activities we can enjoy together.

Creating a Plan

With goals in mind, create a plan to reach them. This is your roadmap or GPS. Break down your long-term goals into manageable short-term tasks.

For example, if you want a better-paying job:

1. Research: Look into fields or roles that align with your skills and interests but offer better compensation.
2. Network: Connect with people in your desired field. Seek advice, mentorship, and job leads.
3. Education: If necessary, pursue further education or certifications that can make you a more competitive candidate.

Staying Committed

Achieving your goals requires commitment. There will be challenges and setbacks, but persistence is key. Remember why you started this journey and keep your vision in sight.

Conclusion

Finding where you want to be in life begins with understanding what you want and where you currently are. Reflect on your passions and needs, set clear goals, create a plan, and stay committed to your path. Just as an inventor turns an idea into reality, you can turn your vision for your life into your lived experience. So where is it that you want to be in life and are you willing to do what it takes to get there?

Chapter Two: Glow in the Dark

In life, it's easy to shine when the spotlight is on us. When people are watching, acknowledging, and appreciating our efforts, it feels natural to give our best. But true character is revealed when we glow in the dark—when we continue to work hard, even when no one is watching, and even when we feel undervalued or underappreciated.

The Power of Integrity

Integrity means doing the right thing, even when no one is looking. It's about maintaining your standards and ethics regardless of the situation. When you give your best effort in every task, no matter how small or unnoticed, you demonstrate a strong sense of integrity.

For instance, as a home health aide, I often work long hours attending to my clients' needs. There are moments when it feels like my efforts go unnoticed, especially when the job feels undervalued and underpaid. However, I remind myself that my work matters deeply to those I care for, even if they don't always express it.

Building Self-Respect

Working hard, even in the shadows, builds self-respect. When you consistently give your best, you develop a sense of pride in your work and in yourself. You begin to understand that your worth is not defined by external validation but by your own dedication and effort.

When you feel underappreciated, it's easy to let your performance slip. But remember, doing your best isn't just for others—it's for you. It reflects the kind of person you are and aspire to be. Every task you complete with excellence, regardless of recognition, contributes to your growth and self-esteem.

Leaving a Legacy

One of the most profound impacts of glowing in the dark is the legacy you leave behind. Strive to leave every situation better than you found it. Whether it's a job, a relationship, or a project, your influence can create a positive ripple effect.

Think about the people you encounter in your work or daily life. Even if they don't explicitly acknowledge your efforts, they are impacted by your dedication. Your commitment to excellence can inspire others to adopt the same mindset, creating a culture of integrity and respect.

Practical Steps to Glow in the Dark

1. Stay Committed to Your Values: Identify your core values and stick to them, even when it's challenging. For me, compassion and dedication are at the heart of my work as a home health aide.
2. Focus on Self-Improvement: Continuously seek ways to improve your skills and knowledge. This not only makes you better at your job but also boosts your confidence.
3. Seek Internal Validation: Recognize your own accomplishments and give yourself credit. Don't rely solely on external praise to feel valued.
4. Set Personal Standards: Hold yourself to high standards in everything you do. Make a habit of asking yourself if you've done your best, regardless of who is watching.
5. Embrace Challenges: See difficult situations as opportunities to demonstrate your resilience and integrity.

Conclusion

Glowing in the dark means working hard and giving your best, even when you feel undervalued and unappreciated. It's about showing the world—and yourself—the kind of person you are. Your dedication and integrity will not only leave a lasting impact on those around you but will also foster your personal growth and self-respect. In every situation, strive to leave it better than you found it, illuminating your path with the light of your unwavering commitment.

Chapter Three: Successfully Uncomfortable

Imagine a plant confined to a small pot. Its roots have no room to spread, its growth is stunted, and it can never reach its full potential. Similarly, we will never know how far we can go or how much we can achieve if we remain within the confines of our comfort zones. To truly grow, we must embrace discomfort and step into new, challenging experiences.

The Nature of Growth

Growth, whether in nature or in life, requires space and the right conditions. A plant needs room to spread its roots and access to sunlight, water, and nutrients to flourish. In the same way, we need to expose ourselves to new environments, ideas, and challenges to reach our full potential.

Living within our comfort zones may feel safe and secure, but it also limits our opportunities for growth. The comfort zone is a psychological state where we feel at ease and in control. However, real progress happens when we push ourselves beyond these boundaries and venture into the unknown.

Embracing Discomfort

Being successfully uncomfortable means welcoming the unease that comes with new experiences. It's about understanding that discomfort is a sign of growth, not a signal to retreat. When we challenge ourselves, we expand our capabilities and discover strengths we never knew we had.

For example, in my role as a home health aide, I often encounter new situations that test my skills and patience. Initially, these challenges can feel overwhelming. But over time, I've learned that facing these difficulties head-on has made me more resilient and capable.

The Benefits of Stepping Outside Your Comfort Zone

1. Personal Growth: Trying new things helps you learn more about yourself and your abilities. It builds confidence and resilience.
2. New Opportunities: Expanding your horizons opens doors to opportunities you might never have considered.
3. Increased Adaptability: The more you push yourself, the better you become at handling change and uncertainty.
4. Enhanced Creativity: New experiences stimulate your mind, fostering creativity and innovation.

Practical Steps to Get Uncomfortable

1. Set Stretch Goals: Aim for goals that are beyond your current capabilities. These should be challenging but achievable with effort and persistence.
2. Seek New Experiences: Try new activities, take on different responsibilities at work, or learn new skills. For me, this could mean exploring specialized training in healthcare or seeking roles with greater responsibilities.
3. Embrace Failure: Understand that failure is a part of the learning process. Each setback is an opportunity to learn and improve.
4. Surround Yourself with Supportive People: Build a network of people who encourage and support you. They can provide guidance and motivation when you face challenges.
5. Reflect on Your Progress: Regularly assess your growth and recognize how stepping out of your comfort zone has benefited you. This reflection can motivate you to continue pushing your boundaries.

Conclusion

To truly grow, we must be willing to be successfully uncomfortable. Just as plants need room to spread their roots and thrive, we need to step outside our comfort zones to reach our full potential. Embrace new challenges, seek out new experiences, and recognize that discomfort is a sign of growth. By doing so, you'll discover just how far you can go and how much you can achieve. Remember, the only way to know how big you can get is to expand your life and try new things.

Chapter Four : Your Word Is Your Bond

In a world where trust and integrity are paramount, your word is one of the most powerful tools you possess. It's a reflection of your reliability and character. When you make a commitment, following through is essential. Failing to do so can damage your reputation and erode the trust others have in you.

The Importance of Keeping Your Word

Your word is your bond. When you say you're going to do something, people expect you to follow through. Consistently honoring your commitments builds trust and respect, while breaking promises can lead to disappointment and mistrust.

Imagine a friend who always says they'll help you move, but never shows up. Over time, you'll stop relying on them and doubt their promises. The same applies in professional and personal settings. Being dependable on your word is crucial for maintaining strong relationships and a good reputation.

The Consequences of Broken Promises

Failing to keep your word can have significant repercussions:

1. Damaged Relationships: Trust is the foundation of any relationship. Breaking promises can strain or even destroy personal and professional bonds.
2. Lost Opportunities: Reliability is a valuable trait in the workplace. If you're seen as unreliable, you may miss out on career advancements and other opportunities.
3. Eroded Self-Respect: Consistently failing to keep your word can lead to a loss of self-respect and confidence.

Building a Reputation of Reliability

To ensure your word is respected and trusted, follow these guidelines:

1. Be Honest and Realistic: Only make commitments you are confident you can fulfill. It's better to be honest about your limitations than to over promise and under deliver.
2. Prioritize Your Commitments: Understand your priorities and manage your time effectively to ensure you can meet your obligations.
3. Communicate Clearly: If unforeseen circumstances prevent you from keeping a promise, communicate this as soon as possible. Offer an explanation and, if possible, propose an alternative solution.
4. Follow Through: Make a habit of completing tasks you've agreed to, no matter how small they may seem. Each completed commitment reinforces your reliability.
5. Reflect on Your Promises: Regularly assess the promises you've made and ensure you're on track to fulfill them. This helps you stay organized and accountable.

Personal Accountability

Personal accountability is a key component of being reliable. It means taking responsibility for your actions and their outcomes. If you make a mistake or fail to keep your word, own up to it. Apologize, learn from the experience, and make amends where possible.

For example, in my work as a home health aide, reliability is crucial. My clients depend on me for their well-being. If I say I'll be there at a certain time or complete a specific task, it's imperative that I do so. Consistently keeping my word not only builds trust with my clients but also enhances my reputation as a dependable professional.

The Long-Term Benefits

Maintaining your word has long-term benefits that extend beyond immediate relationships and opportunities:

1. Enhanced Reputation: A consistent track record of reliability can lead to greater respect and trust from others.
2. Career Growth: In professional settings, being reliable can open doors to new opportunities, promotions, and responsibilities.
3. Stronger Relationships: Trust is the cornerstone of lasting relationships. Being dependable strengthens personal and professional bonds.

Conclusion

Your word is your bond. Being reliable and honoring your commitments is essential for building trust, maintaining relationships, and enhancing your reputation. By making realistic commitments, prioritizing your obligations, communicating effectively, and taking personal accountability, you can ensure that your word is respected and trusted. Remember, your reliability not only affects how others perceive you but also how you view yourself. Consistently keeping your word is a testament to your integrity and character.

Chapter Five: Failing is Not Losing

Failure is often seen as a negative outcome, but it's an inevitable part of the journey to success. Just because you fail at something doesn't mean you're losing. In fact, each failure is a valuable lesson in disguise, showing you what doesn't work and guiding you closer to what does. The key to success is not avoiding failure but learning from it and continually striving to make better decisions.

The Value of Failure

Failure is a powerful teacher. When you fail, you gain insights that success alone cannot provide. It reveals your weaknesses, challenges your assumptions, and pushes you to innovate. Embracing failure as a part of the process allows you to grow and improve.

Consider Thomas Edison, who famously said, "I have not failed. I've just found 10,000 ways that won't work." Edison's relentless experimentation and willingness to learn from failure eventually led to the invention of the electric light bulb. His story illustrates that failing is not losing; it's an essential step toward success.

Learning from Failure

Each failure provides a learning opportunity:

1. Analyze What Went Wrong: Take the time to understand why you failed. Was it a lack of preparation, a flawed strategy, or external factors? Identifying the cause helps you avoid similar mistakes in the future.
2. Adjust Your Approach: Use the insights gained from failure to refine your approach. Be willing to pivot and try new methods.
3. Stay Persistent: Persistence is crucial. Many successful people have faced numerous failures before achieving their goals. The difference lies in their determination to keep going despite setbacks.

Making Decisions Right

Success is not about always making the right decisions; it's about making the decisions right. This means committing to your choices, learning from the outcomes, and continuously improving your approach. Here's how to make decisions right:

1. Commit Fully: Once you've made a decision, commit to it wholeheartedly. Half-hearted efforts often lead to failure.
2. Be Adaptable: Be open to changing your strategy if things aren't working. Flexibility is key to navigating obstacles and finding better solutions.
3. Seek Feedback: Don't hesitate to seek feedback from others. Constructive criticism can provide valuable insights and help you improve.
4. Reflect and Adjust: Regularly reflect on your progress and adjust your plans as needed. This continuous cycle of action, reflection, and adjustment leads to growth and improvement.

Personal Experience

In my career as a home health aide, I've encountered situations where things didn't go as planned. There were times when my efforts to assist a client didn't yield the desired results, or when I felt underappreciated despite my hard work. However, these experiences taught me valuable lessons about patience, communication, and resilience.

For instance, when a particular approach to a client's care plan didn't work, I had to reassess and find alternative methods. Each failure helped me understand my clients better and improve my caregiving skills. Over time, these adjustments made me a more effective and compassionate aide.

The Success Mindset

Adopting a mindset that views failure as a stepping stone to success is crucial. Successful people are not those who never fail, but those who never give up. They understand that failure is not a reflection of their worth but a part of their journey.

1. Stay Positive: Maintain a positive attitude even in the face of failure. Focus on what you can learn and how you can improve.
2. Embrace Challenges: View challenges as opportunities to grow. Each obstacle you overcome makes you stronger and more resilient.
3. Celebrate Progress: Acknowledge your progress and celebrate small wins. This keeps you motivated and reinforces the value of perseverance.

Conclusion

Failing is not losing. Each failure is a lesson that brings you closer to success. By learning from your mistakes, adjusting your approach, and committing to your decisions, you can turn setbacks into stepping stones. Remember, people are successful not because they always make the right decisions, but because they always make their decisions right. Embrace failure as a part of your journey, and let it guide you toward achieving your goals.

Chapter Six: Dangerous Mind

The mind is a powerful tool that shapes our reality. A positive mindset can propel you towards success, while negative thoughts can hold you back. Cultivating a positive outlook and surrounding yourself with supportive friends while keeping your enemies out of mind is crucial for personal and professional growth. Your friends will support and uplift you, whereas your enemies will sow seeds of doubt and hinder your progress.

The Power of a Positive Mindset

A positive mindset influences every aspect of your life. It affects how you perceive challenges, interact with others, and make decisions. Here's how a positive outlook can be a game-changer:

1. Enhanced Resilience: A positive mindset helps you bounce back from setbacks more easily. Instead of dwelling on failures, you see them as opportunities to learn and grow.
2. Improved Health: Positive thinking can lead to better mental and physical health. It reduces stress, boosts the immune system, and promotes overall well-being.
3. Increased Motivation: When you believe in yourself and your abilities, you're more likely to take action towards your goals. A positive mindset fuels motivation and perseverance.

Keeping Your Friends Close

Surrounding yourself with supportive friends is essential. These individuals believe in you, encourage you, and help you stay focused on your goals. Here's why keeping your friends close matters:

1. Emotional Support: Friends provide a listening ear and a shoulder to lean on during tough times. Their support can help you navigate challenges more effectively.
2. Positive Influence: Spending time with positive, motivated individuals can inspire you to adopt similar attitudes and behaviors.
3. Constructive Feedback: True friends offer honest feedback that helps you improve. They celebrate your successes and help you learn from your failures.

Keeping Your Enemies Out of Mind

While it's important to acknowledge criticism and learn from it, dwelling on negative influences can be detrimental. Your enemies, or those who doubt and criticize you without constructive intent, can undermine your confidence and progress. Here's how to keep them out of mind:

1. Focus on Your Goals: Keep your eyes on your objectives and don't let negative comments distract you. Remember why you started and stay committed to your journey.
2. Limit Exposure: Reduce interactions with individuals who consistently bring negativity into your life. Protect your mental space by setting boundaries.
3. Reframe Criticism: If you encounter criticism, try to find any constructive elements in it. If it's purely negative, let it go and focus on feedback from trusted sources.

Practical Steps to Cultivate a Positive Mindset

1. Practice Gratitude: Regularly acknowledge and appreciate the positive aspects of your life. Gratitude fosters a positive outlook and enhances your mood.
2. Set Realistic Goals: Establish achievable goals that motivate you and provide a sense of accomplishment. Celebrate your progress along the way.
3. Engage in Positive Self-Talk: Replace negative thoughts with positive affirmations. Remind yourself of your strengths and past successes.
4. Surround Yourself with Positivity: Engage with people, media, and activities that uplift and inspire you. Avoid sources of negativity that drain your energy.
5. Mindfulness and Meditation: Practice mindfulness or meditation to stay present and reduce stress. These practices help you maintain a calm and positive mindset.

Personal Experience

In my role as a home health aide, maintaining a positive mindset is crucial. There are days when the work is challenging and exhausting, and negative thoughts can easily creep in. However, by focusing on the positive impact I have on my clients' lives and surrounding myself with supportive colleagues, I stay motivated and resilient.

For example, when facing a difficult situation with a client, I remind myself of the times I've successfully handled similar challenges. I seek advice and encouragement from trusted friends and colleagues, which boosts my confidence and helps me approach the situation with a positive attitude.

Conclusion

A positive mindset is a powerful asset that can transform your life. By keeping your friends close and your enemies out of mind, you create an environment that supports your growth and success. Your friends will uplift and encourage you, while your enemies' negativity will no longer hold you back. Cultivate positivity, focus on your goals, and surround yourself with supportive influences. Remember, the mind is a dangerous tool—use it wisely to shape the life you desire.

Chapter Seven: Golden Clock

Time is the most precious resource we have. Unlike money, which can be earned, saved, and spent, time is finite and irreplaceable. The saying, "You can always make more money, but you can never make more time," encapsulates this reality. Every day, we are given 24 hours, and how we choose to spend them determines the quality and trajectory of our lives. The concept of the "golden clock" symbolizes the invaluable nature of time, reminding us to use it wisely and with purpose.

The Irreplaceable Value of Time

Time is a universal constant, marching forward regardless of our desires or actions. It is a resource that, once spent, can never be reclaimed. This makes time more valuable than any amount of money. No matter how wealthy one may be, they cannot buy more time on this Earth. This is especially poignant when we consider the experiences of those who are old or ill, who often wish for more time to live, love, and accomplish their dreams.

The 24-Hour Gift

Each day presents us with a fresh allotment of 24 hours—a gift that should not be taken for granted. Here's how to make the most of this precious resource:

1. Prioritize Wisely: Identify the most important tasks and focus on them first. Prioritizing ensures that you spend your time on activities that align with your goals and values.
2. Avoid Time-Wasters: Recognize and eliminate activities that do not contribute to your well-being or success. This could include excessive screen time, procrastination, or unproductive habits.
3. Plan and Organize: Use tools like calendars, to-do lists, and planners to organize your day. Planning helps you manage your time efficiently and ensures that you accomplish what you set out to do.
4. Balance Work and Leisure: While it's important to work towards your goals, it's equally crucial to allocate time for rest, relaxation, and relationships. A balanced life is a fulfilling life.
5. Learn to Say No: Protect your time by learning to say no to commitments that don't align with your priorities. It's important to set boundaries and avoid over committing yourself.

The Impermanence of Time

The finite nature of time is a reality we must accept. People who are old or sick often realize the value of time too late, wishing they had more of it. This awareness can serve as a powerful reminder to live fully and intentionally. We must cherish each moment, as it is an opportunity that will never come again.

Making Every Moment Count

To truly appreciate the golden clock, we must cultivate a mindset that values time. Here are some principles to guide you:

1. Live in the Present: Focus on the present moment rather than dwelling on the past or worrying about the future. Being present allows you to fully experience and enjoy life.
2. Invest in Relationships: Spend quality time with loved ones. Strong relationships enrich our lives and create lasting memories.
3. Pursue Meaningful Goals: Set and pursue goals that are meaningful to you. Engaging in purposeful activities makes your time feel valuable and fulfilling.
4. Practice Mindfulness: Mindfulness practices, such as meditation, can help you become more aware of how you spend your time and enhance your appreciation of each moment.

The Legacy of Time

How we spend our time not only affects our present but also leaves a legacy. The impact we have on others, the memories we create, and the contributions we make are all reflections of how we chose to spend our time. By valuing and wisely using our time, we create a lasting legacy that can inspire and benefit others.

Personal Experience

In my role as a home health aide, I've witnessed firsthand the preciousness of time. Many of my clients, especially the elderly and those with serious illnesses, often reflect on their lives and the moments they cherished most. Their stories serve as a poignant reminder that time is a gift. I've learned to prioritize meaningful interactions with my clients and spend quality time with my family, knowing that these moments are invaluable.

Conclusion

The golden clock represents the irreplaceable value of time. While money can be earned and spent, time is a finite resource that must be treasured. We each have 24 hours a day, and it's up to us to use them wisely. By prioritizing important tasks, avoiding time-wasters, and living intentionally, we can make the most of our time on Earth. Remember, there are people who are old and people who are sick who cannot buy more time. Cherish every moment, for it is a gift that once gone, can never be reclaimed. Live fully, love deeply, and make every second count.

Chapter Eight: Be Prepared

Opportunities often come unannounced, and being prepared to seize them is crucial. Success is not just about waiting for the right moment but also about being ready when that moment arrives. To make the most of the opportunities that come your way, you need to have the right skills, knowledge, tools, and qualifications. Preparation is the key to turning potential opportunities into tangible successes.

The Importance of Preparation

Preparation is the foundation of success. It equips you with the necessary tools and confidence to tackle challenges and seize opportunities. Without proper preparation, even the best opportunities can slip through your fingers. Here's why being prepared is essential:

1. Confidence: Being well-prepared boosts your confidence. When you know you have the right skills and tools, you approach opportunities with a positive and assured mindset.
2. Competence: Preparation ensures you have the knowledge and competence to perform tasks effectively. This increases your chances of success and reduces the likelihood of mistakes.
3. Readiness: Opportunities can arise unexpectedly. Being prepared means you're ready to act swiftly and decisively, without hesitation or doubt.

Developing the Right Skills and Knowledge

To be prepared, you must continually develop your skills and knowledge. Here are some steps to ensure you're ready when opportunities knock:

1. Identify Relevant Skills: Determine which skills are most relevant to your career or goals. Focus on developing those skills through education, training, and practice.
2. Continuous Learning: Stay updated with the latest trends and advancements in your field. Engage in continuous learning through courses, workshops, reading, and networking.
3. Practical Experience: Gain hands-on experience through internships, volunteer work, or side projects. Practical experience is invaluable in building competence and confidence.

Acquiring the Right Tools

Having the right tools is crucial for effective preparation. Whether it's software, equipment, or resources, ensure you have what you need to perform tasks efficiently:

1. Invest in Quality Tools: Invest in high-quality tools and resources that will help you perform your tasks better. Quality tools can make a significant difference in your productivity and output.
2. Keep Tools Updated: Regularly update and maintain your tools to ensure they are in optimal condition. Outdated or faulty tools can hinder your performance.
3. Learn to Use Tools Efficiently: Take the time to learn how to use your tools effectively. Efficiency with your tools can save you time and improve your results.

Gaining the Right Qualifications

Qualifications can open doors to new opportunities and enhance your credibility. Here's how to ensure you have the right qualifications:

1. Pursue Relevant Certifications: Identify certifications that are valued in your field and pursue them. Certifications demonstrate your expertise and commitment to professional development.
2. Higher Education: Consider pursuing higher education if it aligns with your career goals. Advanced degrees can provide deeper knowledge and open up more opportunities.
3. Professional Associations: Join professional associations related to your field. These organizations offer resources, networking opportunities, and recognition that can enhance your qualifications.

Preparing for the Unexpected

Preparation also involves being ready for the unexpected. Life can be unpredictable, and having contingency plans is essential:

1. Risk Management: Identify potential risks and develop strategies to mitigate them. This helps you stay resilient in the face of challenges.
2. Backup Plans: Always have backup plans in place. If your initial plan fails, a well-thought-out backup plan can keep you on track.
3. Adaptability: Cultivate adaptability and flexibility. Being able to adjust to changing circumstances is a valuable trait that enhances your preparedness.

Personal Experience

In my journey as a home health aide, I've learned the importance of being prepared. Working in healthcare requires not only the right skills and knowledge but also the ability to handle unexpected situations. For instance, I made sure to stay updated with the latest medical practices and obtained relevant certifications. I also invested in quality tools and equipment that helped me perform my duties more efficiently.

One day, an unexpected opportunity arose when a higher-level position became available at my workplace. Because I was prepared with the right qualifications and experience, I confidently applied for the position. My preparation paid off, and I was able to advance my career.Being prepared is essential for seizing opportunities and achieving success. By developing the right skills and knowledge, acquiring the necessary tools, and gaining relevant qualifications, you

Conclusion

position yourself to make the most of any opportunity that comes your way. Preparation boosts your confidence, enhances your competence, and ensures you're ready to act when the moment arrives. Remember, opportunities often come when you least expect them. Stay prepared, stay ready, and you'll be able to turn those opportunities into achievements.

Chapter Nine: Closed Mouths

One of the most important habits you can develop on your path to success is the willingness to ask questions. Closed mouths don't get fed, and in the realm of knowledge and growth, this saying holds especially true. Never be afraid to ask questions because without asking, you'll never get the answers you need. Assuming can lead to mistakes, but asking questions ensures you get it right.

The Importance of Asking Questions

Asking questions is fundamental to learning and understanding. It shows curiosity, a desire to learn, and a commitment to getting things right. Here's why asking questions is crucial:

1. Clarification: Questions help clarify doubts and uncertainties. When you're unsure about something, asking a question can provide the clarity needed to move forward confidently.
2. Avoiding Mistakes: Making assumptions can lead to errors. By asking questions, you can avoid misunderstandings and ensure you're on the right track.
3. Learning and Growth: Every question you ask is an opportunity to learn something new. This continual learning process is essential for personal and professional growth.

Overcoming the Fear of Asking Questions

Many people hesitate to ask questions out of fear of appearing ignorant or bothersome. However, it's important to overcome this fear:

1. Embrace Curiosity: Remember that curiosity is a sign of intelligence, not ignorance. Asking questions shows that you're engaged and eager to learn.
2. Create a Supportive Environment: Encourage a culture where questions are welcomed and valued. Whether in the workplace, at school, or in social settings, creating an environment that supports inquiry benefits everyone.
3. Practice Confidence: Build your confidence by regularly asking questions, starting with small ones. Over time, you'll become more comfortable and assertive in seeking answers.

Asking the Right Questions

Not all questions are created equal. Asking the right questions can lead to deeper understanding and better results. Here's how to ask effective questions:

1. Be Specific: Ask specific questions rather than vague ones. This makes it easier to get precise and relevant answers.
2. Focus on Solutions: Frame your questions in a way that focuses on finding solutions or gaining understanding.
3. Listen Actively: Pay close attention to the answers you receive. Active listening helps you absorb information more effectively and can lead to follow-up questions for further clarity.

The Benefits of Asking Questions

1. Improved Understanding: Questions help you understand complex topics more thoroughly. They allow you to dig deeper and grasp nuances that you might otherwise miss.
2. Enhanced Communication: Asking questions fosters better communication. It shows that you're engaged and interested in the conversation, building stronger relationships.
3. Empowerment: Seeking answers empowers you with knowledge. The more you know, the more confident and capable you become in your endeavors.

Personal Experience

In my career as a home health aide, asking questions has been a vital part of my success. Whether it's understanding a client's medical history, learning new caregiving techniques, or navigating administrative procedures, asking questions ensures I have the information I need to provide the best care possible.

For example, when I was assigned to a new client with a complex medical condition, I made it a point to ask detailed questions about their care requirements, medication schedule, and personal preferences. This not only helped me provide better care but also built trust and rapport with the client and their family.

Encouraging Questions in Others

Fostering a culture where questions are encouraged can have a positive impact on those around you. Here's how to support and encourage questioning:

1. Lead by Example: Demonstrate your own willingness to ask questions. This sets a positive example and encourages others to do the same.
2. Create Safe Spaces: Ensure that people feel safe and respected when asking questions. Avoid judgment and provide constructive feedback.
3. Celebrate Curiosity: Recognize and celebrate the value of curiosity and inquiry. Show appreciation for thoughtful questions and the insights they bring.

Conclusion

Closed mouths don't get fed. Never be afraid to ask questions, as it is through questioning that you gain knowledge, clarity, and understanding. Asking questions prevents mistakes and leads to better decisions and outcomes. Overcome the fear of asking questions, focus on asking the right ones, and create an environment that encourages inquiry. Remember, the only way to find answers is to ask questions. Don't assume—ask, learn, and get it right.

Chapter Ten: I'm Exhausted

In the pursuit of our goals, exhaustion can become a formidable obstacle. It's important to recognize when you're tired and need a break. Rest is essential for rejuvenating your mind and body, allowing you to come up with new and interesting ideas. However, it's equally important not to let rest turn into prolonged inactivity. The balance between rest and perseverance is crucial for maintaining momentum and achieving success.

The Importance of Taking a Break

Taking a break is not a sign of weakness or failure; it's a necessary part of maintaining productivity and creativity. Here's why breaks are important:

1. Mental Rejuvenation: Resting allows your brain to recover from continuous exertion, leading to improved focus and creativity.
2. Physical Recovery: Physical rest is essential for your body to repair and strengthen itself, preventing burnout and fatigue.
3. Stress Reduction: Taking breaks helps reduce stress levels, enhancing your overall well-being and mental health.

Recognizing When You Need a Break

It's important to be aware of the signs that indicate you need a break.
These can include:

1. Decreased Productivity: Struggling to focus or complete tasks
    efficiently can be a sign of mental fatigue.
2. Irritability and Stress: Increased irritability or stress levels can
    indicate that you need to step back and recharge.
3. Physical Symptoms: Headaches, muscle tension, and fatigue are
    physical signs that your body needs rest.

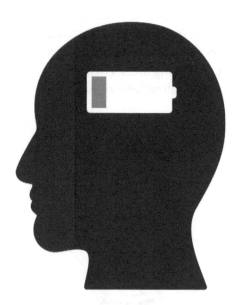

Effective Ways to Rest

Resting effectively involves more than just stopping work. Here are some ways to rest that can help you rejuvenate:

1. Short Breaks: Take short breaks throughout your day to prevent burnout. Even a few minutes of stretching or walking can make a difference.
2. Disconnect: Step away from screens and digital devices to give your eyes and mind a break.
3. Engage in Leisure Activities: Pursue hobbies or activities that you enjoy and that help you relax. Reading, gardening, or listening to music can be excellent ways to unwind.
4. Sleep Well: Ensure you're getting enough quality sleep each night. Sleep is crucial for mental and physical recovery.

The Danger of Resting Too Long

While taking breaks is essential, resting too long can lead to inertia and a loss of momentum. Here's how to avoid the slippery slope of prolonged inactivity:

1. Set Time Limits: Establish a clear time limit for your breaks. This helps ensure you don't rest too long and lose your drive.
2. Stay Engaged: Keep your mind engaged even during breaks. Light activities like reading or solving puzzles can keep your brain active without overexertion.
3. Plan Your Return: Have a plan for getting back to work after your break. Knowing what you'll tackle next can help ease the transition.

Finding the Balance

Striking the right balance between rest and action is key to maintaining productivity and achieving your goals. Here are some tips for finding that balance:

1. Listen to Your Body: Pay attention to your body's signals. Rest when you need to, but stay mindful of how long you're resting.
2. Prioritize Tasks: Focus on high-priority tasks first. This helps you make the most of your energy and time.
3. Schedule Breaks: Incorporate scheduled breaks into your routine. This ensures you take necessary rests without falling into prolonged inactivity.

Personal Experience

In my role as a home health aide, I've experienced the importance of balancing rest and work. Caring for clients can be physically and emotionally demanding, and there have been times when I felt completely exhausted. I learned to recognize the signs of burnout and took short breaks to rest and rejuvenate. I made sure not to let these breaks extend too long, maintaining my commitment to my clients and my goals.

For instance, during particularly challenging days, I'd take a few minutes to step outside, breathe deeply, and clear my mind. This brief respite allowed me to return to my duties with renewed focus and energy, ultimately enhancing the quality of care I provided.

Conclusion

Exhaustion is a natural part of any demanding pursuit, but it doesn't have to derail your progress. Recognize when you need a break and take it to rejuvenate your mind and body. However, be cautious not to rest too long, as it can lead to a loss of momentum. Striking the right balance between rest and perseverance is key to maintaining productivity and achieving your goals. Rest, recover, and keep moving forward. Remember, rest is a tool for success, not a reason to stop.

Chapter Eleven: Goals Versus Dreams

Having goals is essential for personal and professional growth, but without action, they remain just dreams. Goals without action turn into wishful thinking or daydreaming. It's crucial to pursue your goals actively, rather than merely talking about them. Taking action is the biggest step towards turning your aspirations into reality and achieving success.

The Difference Between Goals and Dreams

Goals and dreams are often used interchangeably, but they are fundamentally different:

1. Dreams: Dreams are aspirations or desires that reside in our imagination. They are often vague and lack a concrete plan for realization.
2. Goals: Goals are specific, measurable, attainable, relevant, and time-bound (SMART). They are accompanied by a clear plan of action and steps to achieve them.

The Importance of Taking Action

Taking action is the bridge between your current state and your desired outcome. Here's why action is crucial:

1. Transforms Vision into Reality: Action turns abstract dreams into tangible achievements. Without action, even the best-laid plans remain unrealized.
2. Builds Momentum: Each step you take towards your goal builds momentum, making it easier to continue progressing.
3. Fosters Learning and Growth: Taking action, even if imperfect, allows you to learn from your experiences and grow. Mistakes and setbacks become valuable lessons.

Overcoming Procrastination

Procrastination is a common barrier to taking action. Overcoming it is essential for pursuing your goals:

1. Break Down Goals: Divide your goals into smaller, manageable tasks. This makes them less overwhelming and easier to start.
2. Set Deadlines: Establish clear deadlines for each task. Deadlines create a sense of urgency and help you stay on track.
3. Eliminate Distractions: Identify and minimize distractions that prevent you from taking action. This might involve creating a focused workspace or setting specific times for work.

The Power of Consistency

Consistency is key to achieving your goals. Regular, sustained effort yields better results than sporadic bursts of activity:

1. Create a Routine: Develop a routine that incorporates daily or weekly actions towards your goals. Consistency builds habits and makes progress habitual.
2. Track Progress: Monitor your progress regularly. This helps you stay motivated and make adjustments as needed.
3. Celebrate Milestones: Acknowledge and celebrate small victories along the way. Celebrating progress boosts motivation and reinforces your commitment.

Turning Dreams into Actionable Goals

To turn your dreams into actionable goals, follow these steps:

1. Define Your Dream: Clearly articulate what you want to achieve. Be specific about your aspirations.
2. Set SMART Goals: Break down your dream into SMART goals. Ensure each goal is Specific, Measurable, Attainable, Relevant, and Time-bound.
3. Develop an Action Plan: Create a detailed action plan outlining the steps needed to achieve each goal. Include deadlines and resources required.
4. Take the First Step: Begin with the first step, no matter how small. Taking the initial action is often the hardest part, but it sets the process in motion.

Personal Experience

In my journey as a home health aide, I've learned the importance of taking action to achieve my goals. Early in my career, I dreamed of providing the best care possible for my clients. However, it wasn't until I set specific goals and took concrete steps that I saw significant improvement in my work.

For example, I set a goal to enhance my medical knowledge and skills. I enrolled in relevant courses, attended workshops, and consistently applied what I learned in my daily tasks. Taking these actions not only improved my caregiving abilities but also opened up new opportunities for career advancement.

Staying Committed to Your Goals

Maintaining commitment to your goals can be challenging, but it's essential for success:

1. Stay Focused: Keep your end goal in mind and remind yourself why it's important to you. Visualize the outcome to stay motivated.
2. Be Adaptable: Be willing to adjust your plans as needed. Flexibility allows you to navigate obstacles and stay on course.
3. Seek Support: Surround yourself with supportive people who encourage and motivate you. Share your goals with them and seek their guidance when needed.

Conclusion

Goals without action are just dreams. To turn your aspirations into reality, you must take consistent, deliberate action. Overcome procrastination, create a routine, and stay committed to your goals. Remember, taking action is the biggest step towards success. Transform your dreams into actionable goals, develop a clear plan, and start taking steps towards achieving them. By doing so, you'll turn wishful thinking into tangible accomplishments and realize your full potential.

Chapter Twelve: Be Yourself

True success is deeply personal and can only be achieved when you are authentic to yourself. Living your life and finding your own path is crucial. Following someone else's dream, even if it brings financial rewards, will ultimately leave you unsatisfied. It's important to pursue what genuinely fills you with joy and purpose.

The Importance of Authenticity

Being authentic means staying true to your values, beliefs, and passions. Here's why authenticity is essential for genuine success:

1. Personal Fulfillment: True fulfillment comes from pursuing goals and dreams that resonate with your inner self. When you live authentically, you experience deeper satisfaction and joy.
2. Long-Term Happiness: Authentic pursuits lead to sustained happiness. Achievements that align with your true self provide lasting contentment, unlike superficial successes.
3. Integrity: Living authentically means aligning your actions with your values. This integrity builds self-respect and earns the respect of others.

The Risks of Following Others

Following someone else's path can lead to dissatisfaction and a sense of emptiness, even if it appears successful from the outside. Here are the risks:

1. Lack of Fulfillment: Achieving goals that aren't truly yours can feel hollow. Without personal meaning, success loses its luster.
2. Burnout: Pursuing someone else's dream can lead to burnout, as the effort required doesn't align with your passions or strengths.
3. Regret: Living someone else's life can lead to long-term regret. Looking back, you may feel that you missed out on what truly mattered to you.

Embracing Your Unique Journey

Everyone's journey is unique, and it's important to embrace your individuality. Here's how to celebrate your unique path:

1. Accept Imperfections: Understand that no journey is perfect. Embrace your imperfections and learn from your experiences.
2. Celebrate Differences: Your path may differ from others, and that's okay. Celebrate what makes you unique and appreciate the diversity of experiences.
3. Stay True to Yourself: Resist the pressure to conform to others' expectations. Stay committed to your own values and dreams.

Balancing Practicality and Passion

While it's important to follow your passions, practicality is also necessary. Here's how to balance both:

1. Financial Stability: Ensure you have a plan for financial stability. Pursue your passions in a way that also supports your financial needs.
2. Skill Development: Invest in developing skills that align with your passions. This makes it easier to turn your interests into viable career options.
3. Adaptability: Be open to adapting your path. Sometimes, combining passion with practicality leads to new, fulfilling opportunities.

Personal Experience

In my journey as a home health aide, I discovered the importance of being true to myself. Initially, I considered other career paths that seemed more lucrative.However,I realized that my passion for helping others and making a difference in their lives was where my true fulfillment lay.

By embracing this passion, I found immense satisfaction in my work. Even though the financial rewards weren't as high as in other fields that I had once pursued, the personal fulfillment I experienced was invaluable. This authenticity in my career choice has brought me lasting happiness and a sense of purpose.

Conclusion

Success is not true if it's not achieved for yourself. Live your life authentically and find your own path. Following someone else's dream may bring temporary rewards but will leave you unsatisfied in the long run. Discover what truly fills you with joy and pursue it with dedication. Embrace your unique journey, balance practicality with passion, and stay true to yourself. By being yourself, you'll achieve a success that is deeply meaningful and fulfilling.

Made in United States
Troutdale, OR
01/07/2025

27382974R00056